A Backward Look

A Backward Look

Selected Verse
Clarine Coffin Grenfell

Clarine Coffin Grenfell

wishing Adrienne, joy, wishing

for love, peace, happiness

Additional titles by the same author:
Roses in December
The Caress and the Hurt
Women My Husband Married

This book is an authorized reprint of verse published previously in the above titles.

A Publication of
GRENFELL READING CENTER
Alamoosook Lake
Orland, Maine 04472

ISBN: 0-9612766-3-0

PRINTED IN THE UNITED STATES OF AMERICA BY
LITHOGRAPHICS, INC., CANTON, CT 06019

"Poetry, Mrs. G.? Do we hafta? I hate poetry!"
"Hate poetry? How can you say that? Put your finger on your
    pulse . . . feel the beat? the throb? the rhythm? That's
    *poetry! Why, **you** are a walking poem! You can't hate*
    yourself!"
"A walkin' poem? Me?"

. . . for those hundreds and hundreds of "walking poems," my students,
in whom for some fifty years, 1929 – 1984, I tried to instill the love of
poetry—as if one could!

CONTENTS

130

These are the days when Birds come back —
A very few — a Bird or two —
To take a backward look.

These are the days when skies resume
The old — old sophistries of June —
A blue and gold mistake.

Oh fraud that cannot cheat the Bee —
Almost thy plausibility
Induces my belief.

Till ranks of seeds their witness bear —
And softly thro' the altered air
Hurries a timid leaf.

Oh Sacrament of summer days,
Oh Last Communion in the Haze —
Permit a child to join.

Thy sacred emblems to partake —
Thy consecrated bread to take
And thine immortal wine!

Emily Dickinson

Reprinted by permission of the publishers and the Trustees of Amherst College from
THE POEMS OF EMILY DICKINSON, *edited by Thomas H. Johnson, Cambridge, Mass.: The Belknap Press of Harvard University Press, Copyright 1951,*
© *1955, 1979, 1983 by the President and Fellows of Harvard College.*

Spring

"Always here—the lone loon's aching cry . . . ."

Photo by Robert Mushrall

NINE GRANITE STEPS

When she retired from fifty years in schools
she found a room near the University, and on spring days
drives through McDonald's for a hamburger
a coffee with two creams and one
forbidden chocolate sundae without nuts . . .
parks near the old library, climbs up
laboriously, one at a time
nine granite steps
spreads on the topmost ledge her plastic lunch
and, out of breath, sits down
to munch . . .

Snow is melting fast—a few
black patches here and there, no birds as yet, no leaves
but the breeze is warm and sun feels good upon
arthritic neck, arthritic knees . . .
She lifts her skirt a bit . . .

Behind, are heavy tables where she'd sat,
old books she'd thrilled to—Brooke, and Lawrence Hope
"If I should die, think only this . . ." "Pale hands
I loved beside the Shalimar . . . ."

Before her there beyond the leafless trees
Phi Eta, Delta Tau, and SAE where she'd been happy once—
danced, laughed, been kissed . . .
Is that a robin? No—too soon, and pale March sun
has slipped behind a cloud, the breeze has cooled . . .

Carefully
she packs her paper rubbish—empty cups
two creamers, napkin, spoon—into one bag . . .
climbs down
laboriously, one at a time
nine granite steps
drives home and dozes off
watching the soaps . . . .

10

VIOLETS FOR MY MAMA

For Trelawney Jean Grenfell

When I was a little girl like you,
Five or four or three or two,
One thing in spring I'd always do —
*   Pick violets for my Mama!*

I'd wait for the snow to melt away
Through March and April till early May
When suddenly, near Mother's Day,
*   There'd be violets for my Mama!*

I'd run to pick the bits of sky
Fallen in patches far and nigh,
Wondering why they made her cry,
*   These violets picked for Mama.*

She'd hold them in her hands quite still
While I filled a cup for the window sill,
And always hidden tears would spill
*   On violets picked for Mama!*

But now I know . . . she remembered, too —
Because it's a thing all little girls do —
Once she'd been a child, like me, like you,
*   Picking violets for her Mama!*

So, Lawni, look — are the fields still bare?
Has the blue sky fallen anywhere?
Run quick to pick! Kneel . . . say a prayer
*   For violets and for Mamas!*

FAMILY FUN

Mother saved all year
to take six children to the Bangor Fair
where we each paid a dime to lean over a pit
    watch the **Wild Man of Borneo**
    with black, matted hair
    wearing only a leopard-skin loin cloth
struggle and strain to break thick chains
bound round his hands, his arms, his legs
    giving all the while
    great agonizing growls, blood-curdling screams
that we heard over and over again in nightmares
    way up till Christmas . . . .

Father said, **"Tide's out! Let's go clamming!"**
took us to the ocean to squish hot feet
    in cool mud flats
fish up fat clams with bare black hands
squeeze them hard to make them squirt
souse the slatted basket up and down in white surf
    steam them under seaweed
    over driftwood fires
brought us home at dusk with black fingernails
    pockets full of clam shells
    bellies full of clams . . . .

Mother dressed us in starched white linen
rode us fifteen miles from Bangor to Oldtown
on 'the oldest railroad in the USA'
to stay overnight with our rich Aunt Lillie
    who had no children
    gave us one cookie each for our dessert
and when she showed us her front parlor
    where the conch shells were
    and the dried cocoanuts and the ivory fans
and all the other things brought from China long ago
kept saying: **"Don't touch! Don't touch! Don't touch!"**

Father said, **"Blackberries are ripe! Fetch lard pails!"**
walked us across warm meadows
    yellow with goldenrod, orange with Susans

blue with asters, red with paintbrush
showed us how to whistle on a blade of grass
suck a piece of timothy when we were thirsty
carried the youngest home on his back
gave us heaping bowls of his berries for our supper
> *to eat with yellow cream*
> *purple tongues, purple teeth*
because our berries had all disappeared on the way . . . .

Mother wound our hair in white cotton rags
brushed corkscrew curls around her finger
fastened white ribbon hairbows on each head
buttoned shoes too small on feet too big
> *walked us long miles*
> *all the way downtown to Perry's Studio*
> *where a man put a beautiful toy in our hands*
> *a white-painted horse*
with red-painted wheels and a horsehair tail
> *to hold for just one minute*
while he went under a big black cloth, yelled
> ***"Smile! Look happy!"***
and sent us limping home in our too-small shoes . . . .

And yellowing away in a drawer somewhere
I have the picture of that solemn child
> *with the stiff, tight curls*
> *and the high-buttoned shoes*
> *clutching the toy that wasn't hers*
And when I come across it, I think of the mother
> *who worked so hard, so very hard*
> *to give six children all the things*
> *they didn't need and didn't want . . . .*

But the picture of the child
with purple tongue, muddy hands
wild curls tangled with breezes from the sea
tossed high in the air by a laughing Dad
caught, held safe in strong, sure arms
> *that picture I look at often and smile because*
> *it is in my heart, shiny and bright forever . . . .*

IN THE SPRING

I want to be in love in the spring—
Not a vulgar body passion
That consumes, devours, destroys,
But a tender little love, like a flower . . .

Someone to walk with
Through the hazy twilight . . .
Someone to talk with
Using no words . . .
Someone who'll be quiet
When evening stars are dawning,
Wish on Lady New Moon,
Laugh, and kiss my hair . . .

Someone, will you hurry?
Tulip bugles call you!
Spring is not for laggards—
Someone, come!

COINCIDENTAL DAY

April 3, 1931

It was, of course, by chance we met that day.
By happenstance — an unexpected cut,
Some stationery needed, bookstore near,
And there you were, standing with book in hand,
A tall, slim boy I'd known through college years
Only by name, quite casually. You turned,
Put book back on the shelf, said **"Hi,"** *and smiled.*
"Oh, hi — what are you reading?"
                                  "Anything —
Except religion. I've no use for that."
"An atheist, then?"
                     "Almost —" *And so we talked*
Awhile of God, condescendingly, until
The clerk put stationery in my hand.
"Must go — write a letter for the mail."

                                   All chance,
Of course. All happenstance. And did He smile ,
The Omniscient One, that coincidental day,
As we dismissed him in our cavalier way —
And is He smiling still? — hearing you say
Offhandedly, **"I'll walk along with you**
A little way, if I may . . . a little way . . . ."

                  April 3, 1981

I NEVER KNEW

I never knew of love
Until
That night in May beneath the stars
When misty moonlight drifted through
The needles of the pines
And older needles, brown and scented, made for us
A warm and fragrant bed . . .

I never knew of love
Until
Upon my full warm breast you laid
The fullness of your lips and swore that you were mine
While high and sweet the peepers played
Our wedding march
For I married you then
Your soul and mine in holy radiance and bliss
Became as one . . .

It matters not
What other man may place
A golden circlet on my hand . . .
I have been bride
To you and you alone
Are my true mate . . .
Through all the years close-pressed
Adored
I love you

ON MONUMENTS

We lay on the riverbank that final day,
Remembering the springtime hours we'd shared,
Counting them one by one, and reaching out
Pried pebbles from wet sand, one for each hour . . .
Like playful children then laid stone on stone
Until we'd built a kind of pyramid —
Uneven, frail, a fragile monument
To youth and joy and love, to hopes and dreams
Far off, more fragile still — then clasping hands,
Kissed lightly one last time and walked away.

The world has countless monuments — Stonehenge,
Sphinx, Eiffel Tower, the marble David white
In the bright Italian square, the supine slave
That altered Schweitzer's life, the Taj Mahal . . .

Why, then, when I think of monuments, do I
See only a little heap of tide-washed stones,
Wavery, unsure, a wobbly pyramid
Built long ago by an artless boy and girl
Who count shared hours, then kiss, and hand in hand,
Their faces toward each other, walk away . . . .

THE HAND

The hand that stopped writing
Hangs there
Over the arm of the flowered chair
In the snapshot you sent at Christmas . . .

I remember that hand, remember it well—
Carrying books,
Rifling pages, searching for sonnets . . .
'Bright Star, would I were steadfast as Thou art . . .'
At the box office, proffering bills,
Holding my coat, black velvet,
Opening doors, menus,
Tamping a pipe,
Leaning on bridges,
Lifted high, pointing at stars . . .

I remember that hand, remember it well—
Clearing the ground,
Tucking in blankets,
Picking a flower,
Lifting my chin,
Touching tears,
Smoothing my hair,
Reaching for pebbles,
Waving goodbye . . .

I remember that hand,
The hand hanging there
Over the arm of the flowered chair . . .
Remember it well—
The hand that stopped writing.

ASTRONOMY I — THE LONG, LONG COURSE

The first time ever we walked beneath the stars —
A million stars, a million years ago —
You stretched your arm straight up and gave me one:
"That's our star! Two points off the bow of Delta Tau!"
Then swung my arm round till I found it, too.
"By the triangle?"
              "No, sweet! Not a triangle!
Just two big stars and a little one — ha, ha!"

So we argued names, discarded Latin, Greek,
Chose a simple honest name and nickname, too,
*And you said, **"Now hang on, sweet! Hold tight! Tonight***
We'll fly right up and say 'Hello' to Osc!"

So you kissed me then, and up, up, up we flew
Past a million other stars to claim our own —
'For better or for worse, for rich or poor,
In sickness, health' *— till we kissed our last goodbye.*
"Don't say 'Goodbye' — say 'See you later, dear!'
When you look at Oscar, I'll be looking, too!"

So I looked . . . and looked . . . through a million lonely nights,
*Humming Hoagy's song: **'Sometimes I wonder why —'***
*Looked **'two points off the bow'** when Delta Tau*
Was a million, million lonely miles away . . .

And so, my sweet, were you, and I never did
'See you later, dear,' *and, no, there never was*
'A little one — ha, ha!' *Still, I had a star.*
I had a star. I always had a star.
Good times or bad, glad times or sad, always
I had a star. I had a special star —
A special, distant, cold, uncaring star
That a faithless sweetheart picked from a million stars
And gave with a faithless kiss on an April night
A million, million, million years ago . . . .

MEA CULPA

You tell me:
"Make a little image out of wax, wax, wax
And buy a little box all full of pins, pins, pins
And every time you think of me, stick one in . . . ."

Every time . . .
          I go for the mail
          or cross the bridge
          or walk in the rain

Every time . . .
          I read a poem
          or see the new moon
          or wish on a star

Every time . . .
          I meet a boy and a girl
          walking hand in hand
          the wind in their hair

Every time . . .
          I glance at the stands
          the topmost row
          where you first said the words

Oh, I'll make a little image out of wax, wax, wax
And I'll buy a little box all full of pins, pins, pins
And every time I think of you, I'll—

Need lots and lots of pins, my darling . . .
                    boxes . . .
                        and boxes . . .
                            and boxes . . .
                                of pins . . . .

JAPE

Gods on your mountains, were you bored with all
Life's other merry jests that you should please —
When I was peaceful, when I was content —
To lift me for one windswept day into
Your radiant company, show me all light,
All laughter, and all love only to tire
Of my too naive joy and fling me back
Into the commonplace?

And was it as a kind of souvenir
Or payment for your quite amusing jape
That you should leave upreaching empty arms
And eyes from viewing light too bright struck blind?

O gods, I do not beg. Too well I know
That life on mountain heights is yours, not mine.
This only tell: why was I shown the light?
And how, knowing what life could be, am I
To live it as it all too surely is?

LIGHTED HOURS

We shared together only simple joys —
The moonlit sea, red sunset through the trees,
A certain star — for always strangely sweet
And natural seemed our two souls' company.
Our love was not for words. Only to know
The aching grip of strong, lean hands sufficed,
Or meet your eyes across the candlelight
And feel myself like flame-touched wax dissolve.

It may be we shall never meet again,
But I'll remember you. Though many days
And scenes both near and far shall come between,
I'll not forget. Life brings its lighted hours
Whose loveliness and warmth into the gloom
Of soon-forgotten things fade not away.

So on all mountain tops and by all seas
And when all ships creep silent past the moon,
I'll think of you and love you tenderly.

ONCE

We had it once
The joy, the walk-on-air
The oh-what-a-wonderful-world, the ecstasy
All ours
A few brief halcyon days
And if
We lost it there
Somewhere
Along the way
No matter, dear
Be glad
We had it once.

ALWAYS

Always the thought of you, my love,
Always the thought of you—
Deep in my heart where I truly live
Always the thought of you . . .

Under the myriad words I say,
The myriad things I do,
Tender and warm in my hidden heart
Always the thought of you . . .

Always the memory of your face,
The eyes, the hands I knew—
Lighting my life from a secret place
Always the thought of you . . .

THINGS SEEM DIFFERENT AT EASTERTIDE

Things seem different at Eastertide
When someone dear to you has died.
You think very little about what you'll wear,
But you listen to the preacher when he speaks in prayer.
Yes, things seem different at Eastertide
When someone close to you has died —

You look at the lilies, pure white from blackest earth,
And you think about death and you think about birth,
And you say, "Christ Jesus, is it really true?
Does he live? Is he living, somewhere with you?
Those 'heavenly mansions' you went to prepare —
Are they real? Shall I know him someday there?"

Yes, things seem different at Eastertide
When someone dear to you has died.

THEN I REMEMBER

Sometime it seems so far away,
That first triumphant Easter Day,
I feel it scarcely real somehow,
So more real is the here and now.

Then I remember with a chill
That Golgotha is any hill,
Jerusalem is any town —
Maybe He's here now, looking down.

Then I remember with a start
Judas may live in any heart
That harbors jealousy or greed,
That's hypocrite in word or deed.

So to my knees I go in prayer
At an altar rail or anywhere
And say, "Christ Jesus, forgive me, too!
I'm one of those who crucified you!

I'm one of those who came and sat,
Spent the three long hours in idle chat!
I'm one of those who just passed by
And said, 'Well, well, we all must die.'

I'm one of those who mocked and railed
And wondered why God's power had failed.
O Master of Life, forgive me, too,
And send me forth Thy will to do!"

SONG OF THE VIKING'S DAUGHTER

And will I marry you, my love,
And will I e'er be true?
I cannot tell, my love, until
I see the sea with you . . .

Until I stand beside your side
To hear great breakers roar
In endless foaming impotence
Against the endless shore . . .

Until I lie beside your side
To watch the white gulls write
Their lovely curving messages
Across the sky in white . . .

Until I know that your heart swells
As mine with almost pain
To feel the wind fill out a sail
And give it life again . . .

For Viking blood is in my veins,
In my heart wanderlust!
Since I shall love the sea alway,
The man I marry must!

And will I marry you, my love,
And will I e'er be true?
I cannot tell, my love, until
I see the sea with you.

THE LIGHTS OF LOVE

I met you in the sunlight, love,
One April day, all green, all blue.
The sunbeams seemed to dance with you,
Entranced with you, as I was, too,
When first we met, my love!

We laughed beneath the starlight, love,
Flinging our gladness to the sky,
Knowing our love could never die.
We heard the stars on high reply
When first we laughed, my love!

By moonlight we first kissed, my love,
A kiss so soft upon my hair
The west wind might have left it there,
A token from the fairest fair
In all the world, my love!

In candlelight we married, love.
I see again the tall flames shine.
I hear again the vow divine
That made thee mine, and me all thine
For all the years, my love!

By firelight we'll grow old, my love,
Your hand in mine for aye and aye
Until all earth lights fade away
In dawning ray of endless day
When we are old, my love!

ALWAYS THE SOMETHING ELSE

These raw March days — trees leafless, frozen ruts
Scarring the barren earth, no singing birds —
I remember how you used to long for spring.

Coming in cold, dragging the heavy bags,
You'd sigh and say, "I wish the spring would come!"
And later when white crocuses pushed up
And daffodils and pale blue hyacinths,
You'd stand by the kitchen door: "I think I'll take
A little ride out in the country, dear —"
Wanting me to answer, "Wait! I'm coming, too!"

Why didn't I? . . . Willows were hanging pale . . .
The hedges sunny with forsythia . . . buds
On the maple trees exploding red . . . why?

Always the something else — the bills to pay,
Letters to write, the cleaning, phoning, meals . . .
No time for looking, dreaming, holding hands . . .
In spite of Housman's poem, no time for spring
And blossoming cherry trees . . . no time for love.

Oh, I'll plant pansies by your stone, come May.
Small velvet faces will look up at me
Reproachfully, for spring will always come —

But never again for you, my dearest dear . . .
And never again with you . . . never with you.

Summer

". . . or paddle out halfway across the lake
To wait the rising moon, to hear loons call."

Photo by David Jefferson

LET ME WALK WITH YOU

Let me walk with you sometimes when you walk alone
On summer days, my hand inside your arm . . .
Imagine me there, my step matching your own,
The sun on our faces, radiant and warm.

Only one plume of breath will rise in the frosty night
If I come with you when the harvest moon hangs low;
Only one set of footprints show in the pristine white
If together we go through softly falling snow.

Do not pause alone by the darkening wood to hear
In the springtime dusk the hidden whippoorwill.
Do not wait alone for the first pale star to appear
As the last red glow fades slowly from the hill.

Let me walk with you. None but you will know I am there —
Only turn when you hear your name and touch my hair.

NEVER A JUNE

Never a June but I remember, dear,
When pine trees lift white candles to the sky
And leaves unfurl, all new, all tender green,
Never a June when lilac blooms but I
Remember — once I called you, and you came.

I called you once in need, in blinding hurt
None but the very young can ever know —
Never a June but I remember, dear —
I called you once in turmoil, and you came . . .
Came instantly, asking no questions, made
A world within the circle of your arms,
A world all safe, wherein I was enclosed.

When leaves hang tremblingly and lilac bloom
Perfumes the warm, sweet air, never a June
But I remember, dear, you held me close
Until my heart was stilled against your own,
And smoothed my hair, and kissed my tears away
On such a day, on such a bright June day . . .

Never a June when tapers on the pines,
All slim, all slender white, light up the sky,
Never a June but I remember, dear,
Though other Junes have come and gone and I
Have solace found in other arms than yours . . .

Till no leaf stir for me, nor lilac bloom,
And candles can no longer light my dark,
Never a June but I'll remember, dear —
I called you once in anguish and in pain.
I called you — and you came, you came, you came.

SINGLE

I have been lonely for you all my life,
Missing you always, wishing I were your wife—
     Longing to share your laughter, grief, or care,
     Your joy is all things beautiful and fair,
     Turning to see your face and no one there . . .

I have been lonely for you all my life,
Wanting you, needing you, wishing I were your wife—
     Needing your strength when there was much to bear,
     Needing your faith when there was much to dare,
     Reaching to touch your hand and touching air . . .

This word, if no other word I write, is true:
I have been lonely all my life for you . . .
     The innermost me that was meant to be your wife
     Has been lonely for you, lonely all my life.

THE OLD, OLD MATH

     Lonely as I could not be, my love,
     Had I your sweet completion never known;
     Lonely as white pen is lone above
     Deserted sea whence her loved cob has flown.

     The ship yearns not for harbor never seen,
     Nor lowlander for mountain height unscaled.
     The sunless cavern, missing not the sheen
     Of light on waves, joys in its shadows veiled.

     But I, my love, have known your arms at night,
     Have heard your heartbeat, drawn a mingled breath.
     Mine is the darkness of remembered light;
     Mine is the conscious and the living death.

     Two become one. Yet, tear the one in twain,
     How strange there should not two, but halves remain!

NOT TRUE

You say you can't remember, dear, that I
Must have forgotten, too, the **where,** the **why,**
The **when** of how we fell in love, we two —
       Not true, not true.

Here in old age, you say, I can't recall
A certain bridge, a certain waterfall,
A night beside the sea when our love grew —
       Not true, not true.

I must, you say, have written it somewhere,
The feeling of your lips upon my hair,
The tender touch of hands that I once knew —
       Not true, not true.

I must have quite forgotten, too, you say,
The way your laughter rang, the endearing way
Your voice broke when you first said, "I love you —"
       Not true, not true.

But — will I remember till the day I die
Our sweet, young love, and do I wish that I
Could sometimes share that memory with you?
       Now that, my love, is true. All true.

"BEDROOM AT ARLES"

Everyone knows you were insane, Van Gogh.
Quite lunatic, yet sane enough to know
The antediluvian truth old Noah knew —
In this mad world all things go two by two —

And so arranged and painted them that way:
Two open windows letting in the day,
Two pillows on the bed, two yellow chairs,
Even the pictures hung in fecund pairs . . .

Yet no one there sets chair straight to the wall,
Or plumps the pillows up, no one at all,
And though the spread is passionately red,
No one waits there, impatient on the bed.

Small wonder, lone Van Gogh, you came undone
When of all your furious works, we bought but one.

THE TRUE, THE DIFFERENT VIEW

For Georgia O'Keeffe

I see you walking city streets at night
On Stieglitz' arm, face tilted toward the light
Of distant stars, a full white moon that you
Will keep from ever waning, ever new . . . .

Near Taos now you gaze into far space . . .
Badlands, wastelands, a desolate barren place
You'll paint in blue, red, yellow, purple, green—
Bright colors none but you had ever seen . . . .

Now you hold a shell, a wild flower in your hands—
Now pry a long-dead skull from desert sands—
Finding in each life's lovely symmetry
Unseen until you paint and make us see.

Our universe is changed because of you
Who give blind eyes the true, the different view.

KNOWLEDGE

I would know your lips
though I could see no face . . .

would know your arms
ten thousand years from now . . .

would know your voice,
though it called through endless space . . .

would know and come to you . . .
somewhere, somehow . . . .

AFTER THE DREAM

I keep my eyes closed a long while
       after the dream . . .
       not wanting to lose you
       not wanting to let you go . . . .

I keep my eyes closed a long while
       after the dream
       remembering your face
       young, vulnerable
       wet with tears
       cradled in my shoulder . . . .

I keep my eyes closed a long while
       after the dream
       willing you to stay
       willing you not to leave me . . . .

UNHEALED

Strange that the wound is unhealed
after all these years . . .

that the hurt never quite goes away,
never quite disappears . . .

that the heartache and pain are still there
and the useless tears. . . .

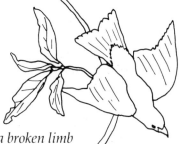

MYSELF SET FREE

Halfway down the maple tree a broken limb
Hangs on year after year, resisting wind,
Rain, snow, and ice . . . resisting time.
                                Grotesque—
Small branches pointing down, not up—it clings
Unnatural, destroying symmetry . . . .

I think of you who loved all trees: "We will trust
Our love so long as it can bear us up."
It broke, of course—could not sustain the weight
Of separation, loneliness, cold ink—
Came crashing down, but halfway only, clings,
Destroying peace, destroying harmony . . . .

I'll call the nurseryman. He'll bring sharp saws,
Sever and cut, set free the shackled tree,
Leave wood for me. I'll kneel to lay the fire,
Place on each long-dead stick a memory,
Then strike the match . . . and stand—myself set free.

WHEN THEY WERE SMALL

Pamela

Oh, the joy of Pam, aged two,
Finding where blueberries grew
Low on bushes, close to shore —
　　"More cherries, Mommy! Pam pick more!"

Small hands reaching, brown eyes keen,
Distinguishing the blue from green,
First sweet taste of Nature's store —
　　"More cherries, Mommy! Pam pick more!"

Nana's Camp
Long Pond, Maine, 1950

John Millard

My little boy is going on four
Isn't a baby anymore
Slams in and out and bangs the door
And 'asking permission' is a bore —
Now he's most four!

The baby smile now is a real boy's grin
With a gleam in the eye of original sin
And the noise he makes an unholy din
As he runs on the lawn where the grass has been —
Now he's most four!

But sometimes, still, there's a special joy
When he forgets he's a great big boy
Lays his head on his mother's knee
As he used to do when he was three
Lets himself be loved one minute more . . .
Then off again with a shout and a roar
To the Grown-up Land, the Big Boy Land

of Four.

Bethel, Connecticut, 1945

Lornagrace
Only been six for a little while
Innocent eyes that know no guile
Sweet lips curved in a shy half-smile
    My flower girl . . . down the aisle

Floats in organdy, three yards wide
Pink taffeta on the underside
Scattering roses for the bride
    My flower girl . . . down the aisle

Little finger cocked high in the air
Drops each petal with a flair
As if to say, **"Bride, step right there!"**
    My flower girl . . . down the aisle

Whispers a secret with high glee:
"I'll be in two weddings, Daddy, see?
This one for Ginny, another for me!"
    My flower girl . . . down the aisle

             Bayside, New York, 1950

STILLBORN

Two little hands clutch at my heart,
Clutch at my heart and always will—
Hands of a baby that once lived
And now are still, forever still.

Our Father, when at last I come
To heaven, if it be Thy will,
May Thy smallest angel welcome me
With hands that I remember still.

New York
Christmas Eve, 1951

BELIEVERS

When Lorni was five, I took her to see **Peter Pan,**
And as, leaning forward, perched on the edge of her seat,
She clapped wildly, wildly, that Tinker Bell live, not die,
Suddenly, in that very moment, dear,
After years of forgetting, I remembered you —
The only man I ever knew who believed
In fairies, too —

                        Queen Mab, Titania, all
Puck's mischievous madcap crew were real to you,
Wee folk we only feel, not see, in mist,
Moonbeam, rainbow, and tree —

                                "Clap!" Peter begged,
A sob in his husky voice as the tiny light
Grew fainter, flickered, died . . .
                                **"Clap! If you
Believe!"** And I felt my daughter tug my sleeve —
"Clap harder, Mommy! Harder, please!" Blue eyes
Ablaze with fear and tears, she beat small hands
Together frantically . . .

                        She believes, I thought,
She could be his child, his spirit child . . . and felt
My own tears, burning hot, and then I, too,
Leaned forward, clapping wildly, wildly, not —
For fairies, but for days we knew when life
Was young, and love was true, and I believed
With all my heart — yes, I believed in you.

CLAH-RA-INE

Playful, you change my name to Navajo.
Will you then be my shaman? Paint for me
Bright images in sands of memory?
Pound into powdered rock our yesterdays?
Call down old gods? Depict the great events —
Your word, your touch, the laughter in your eyes —
That changed a life? Work holy charms that cure?

I am in need of healing. Bending low,
Here at the circle's edge I bow me down,
Wounded in spirit, broken . . . make me whole!
Grant me the central place, the heart's deep core . . .
Enfold me, hold me there a little time
And make for me the magic mandala . . . .

Let twirling fingers swirl the colored sands —
Draw darkness, light . . . red sunset, dawn . . . white mist
In deepest canyon, high on mountain peak,
Above still pool, on crashing waterfall . . .
Oh, reconcile the harsh polarities!
Draw ice! Draw fire! Rejection and desire!
Show thunder in the snow, warm springtime rain . . .
Show blossoming tree and windblown, dying leaf . . .
Meeting and parting . . . pain and ecstasy . . .
Great eagle, soaring, small bird near at hand . . .
Firefly ephemeral, far steadfast star . . .
And sing with star, bird, tree the age-old chant —
The song of joy the morning stars began!
The song of love that made the universe!

Thus seeing, hearing, I may yet be well,
May rise from death to life healed by the touch
Of old shared memory, may walk again
The shimmering rainbow trail . . .
                              I ask because
You change my name and call me Navajo —
And walked the trail with me once long ago.

OURS

School by the bend in the river
Our school
Blue water, tide in
Marsh grass, tide out
Boats frozen in ice
Bundled for winter
And always a salt breeze blowing
Always the gulls
Swooping low over the patio
Flying high
Past field and track

> *Our school*
> *Ours*
> *Orange leaves in fall covering the walks*
> *Red-gold, rustling*
> *Snow banked high in winter*
> *Bending the spruces*
> *Through open windows in spring*
> *The daydreaming smell of lilacs*

> > *Our school*
> > *Bedford*
> > *Red brick, white trim, blue sky*
> > *Under*
> > *Red stripes, blue ground, white stars*
> > *American*
> > *Noisy, rambunctious, free*
> > *Our school*

TEACHER

*"**Read us your poem.**" He waits expectantly,*
Ignores the trembling voice, the nervous hand,
The trochee where the anapest should be,
Mixed metaphor, and meter poorly scanned.

Leaning, he seems to fan the feeble verse,
To cup not only ear, but heart and mind
Around each flickering word, as though to nurse
A blazing flame from fire too long confined.

His eyes intent, his manner kind and mild,
He listens lovingly, as one extends
Both hands toward a toddling child
*And calls '**Come walk! You can** . . .' The poem ends.*

What will the teacher say? A silence, then —
*"**Well, now, that's fine!**" The poet breathes again.*

TEACHING AT HALL

When we did **Beowulf,** we had a Mead Hall
    heated cider in the Home Ec room
    stirred in honey
    pretended to be tipsy
And Mike Kaye put up signs all over the room:
    BED AND BOARD — 1 shilling
    BED AND BAWD — 2 shillings
And for one whole week everyone called the teach
Grendel, Dragon Mother . . . .

And when we read **Two Cities,** the girls brought in
    steel needles, red wool
    sat knitting long scarves
    hating DeFarge, adoring Carton
Until exam day, when everyone came in shouting,
"It was the worst of times!"
And for a month before **Native,** we saved all our bones —
steak bones, chicken bones, fat greasy ham bones —
and on November 5th built a great bone-fire,
    danced around it, tossed on bones,
    shrieking, yelling, **"A Penny for the Guy!"**
till a neighbor called the fire department and the police . . .

And when we did **C and P,** no one could remember
how the vowels went in Dostoievski's name
    till Nan Slonim shouted,
    "O I E V — Oh, I Enjoy Vodka!"
    and after that no one forgot . . . .

And when Camus was killed in his little sports car,
Everyone was quiet because we all knew
    something beautiful and existential
had gone from the world forever
and some of us read **Fall** over again . . . .

And when **Camelot** came to the Bushnell, we went
    because of JFK and because
    Once and Future was our favorite book . . .
And when Yale did **Macbeth**, we went
    90 of us, through a blizzard . . .

*And when B.U. did **Crucible,** we went,*
and there was Arthur Miller in the fifth row with the wife
after Marilyn . . . .

And the day before vacation
when all Stanley's choirs went up and down the corridors
*singing **Deck the Halls** and **Joy to the World***
Elaine Rosenstein and Mimi Fogelman
stood in the doorway of 212
tears streaming down their cheeks because, they said,
"We're seniors. It's our last Christmas!"

And on New Year's Eve there was always Open House
at 612 Fern and last year's seniors
came back from Yale and Brown and Smith
and Holyoke and Harvard and Rensselaer
to show off a bit, and because it's always good
to have a place
to come back to . . .
And everyone laughed and talked and ate
the chocolate birthday cake Joan Shapiro always brought
for Mrs. G.
who went to bed happy that night because, they told her,
"You taught us all the right things.
Other kids know the titles, but you made us
read the books . . . ."

And W.H.H.H.S.
under Rives and Dunn
and Stearns and Leavitt and Robinson and Dyber
Hoffman and Fraser and Freer and Schwendenwein
Richards and DiFrancesco, Deacon and Moore
and five dozen others equally good
was a hard-working school
a proud school
a great school
because all those people happened to like kids
and teaching at Hall
was fun . . . .

WOMEN OF GOD

To a woman first God did impart
The bursting secret of His heart,
And a woman cried, "I am most blessed!"
As God's Son stirred beneath her breast.
Women followed all the way Christ trod,
Climbed the hills to learn of God,
Brought their babies to be blessed,
Haltingly their sin confessed,
Sacrificed their ointments rare,
Dried His feet upon their hair,
Till, in the shadow of the Cross,
Women wept and knew their loss.

Who came early at break of day?
Who found the death stone rolled away?
Who heard when shining angels said,
"Why seek ye the living among the dead?
Your Lord is risen! Do not fear!
Your Lord is risen! He is not here!"
Who ran to tell with trembling voice
*God's great, glad news: **"He lives! Rejoice!"***

Only a vision? An idle tale?
Two thousand years do not prevail
Against that truth!

And are God's lips sealed?
Has He no word to be revealed?
No waiting message to impart
This day unto the quiet heart?
False gods cry loud. Beneath their din
The still, small voice yet speaks within.
Who, listening, hears? Who will proclaim
That voiceless truth in Mary's name?
Denying self, forsaking all,
Who follows now the Master's call?

O women of God who in silence pray,
Rise and herald the truth this day!
To women of old and your God, be true!
Let Christ live in the world through you!

MILKWEED IN FALL

Will God, Who hides inside each pod
Seeds for a hundred springs,
Neglect to send, when my fall comes,
The necessary wings?

Fall

*"Lonely as white pen is lone above
Deserted sea whence her loved cob has flown."*

COMMUNICATION SKILLS

There is a way of speaking
With no word . . .
A way of conversing
With nothing heard . . .

There is a way of talking
Without sound . . .
The old way of telling
Lovers found . . .

An ancient telepathy
Known to the wise
Who send clear messages
From silent eyes . . . .

LIGHTLY IN FALL

Lightly in fall a red clay path we trod,
Crossed brittle fields, then climbed a hill to find
A high cathedral in the lofty pines . . .
Talked there awhile of poems and God and things
Until the lifeblood of the dying day
Stained the green needles of the murmuring choir,
Then homeward turned, and knew that we were one—
     One in the crimson of the dying day . . .
     One in the harmony of swaying trees . . .
     One in the muffled heartbeat of the dusk . . .

We spoke few words, and hand had scarce touched hand,
Yet with a passion half-divine we knew
That far beyond the sunset's reddest hue
Our trembling souls lay one upon God's breast—
Knew, and did not care about the rest.

ELF

For Miranda Katherine Smith

Miranda is a fairy, a leprechaun, a sprite,
A tiny Cornish pesky with a wide, wide smile!
She dances like a moonbeam, a butterfly, an elf,
And all the while her laughing eyes beguile!

TAOISM FOR RHYMESTERS

If you were here, sweet love, there'd be no time
For dallying with rhythm or with rime,
For tapping syllables—now which is best?
Dactyl or trochee? iam? anapest?

If you were here, sweet love, there'd be no need
For scribbling sonnets none will ever read.
We'd find a far, far better thing to do
Than sounding accents, tapping two by two.

Oh, when you come, sweet love, these eager lips
Will be on yours, not pursed on pencil tips.
From dawn till dark, sweet love, sweet love we'll make,
Then sleep, and make sweet love when we awake.

Until that time this foolish verse I fling
Into the void, hoping to make it sing.

GODDAUGHTER, GRANDDAUGHTER

For Clara Beatrice Bowron

Clara Beatrice Bowron, 10,
of Kansas City, MO,
. . . gets up at 5 a.m. to watch the confluence of the planets
. . . feeds her dog Barkis, eats her egg-on-toast, arrives at
prestigious Sunset Hill School for Girls at 8
. . . goes to six classes, gets five A's, and one B +
. . . takes part in a gymnastics show where she excels in
> *knee bends*
> *head stands*
> *balance beam*
. . . comes home at 3, curls her beautiful blonde hair on her
mother's electric curling iron without burning either neck or
fingers
. . . walks briskly to Central United Methodist for
> *acolyte practice at 4*
> *choir practice at 5*
> *church supper at 6*
> *a musical play, **The Babble of Babel,** at 7,*
> *in which she, of course, has the lead and so*
. . . bows graciously when presented a long-stemmed American
Beauty rose from one of her many male admirers
. . . arrives home at 9, full of vim, vigor, and vitality, asking only
"What's to eat?"
. . . lays out clothes for the morrow, says prayers, goes to sleep.

Clara Beatrice Bowron, 10,
of Kansas City, MO,
goddaughter, granddaughter
is quite a girl.

I asked her once, when we were having a picnic on the White House
*lawn, **"Would you like to live here?"***
"Oh," *she replied nonchalantly, **"I suppose I might be**
President someday."*

EMPTY PLACES

For James Edgar Bowron, III

When I glance at the lake on a summer day and see
Far out, bobbing on the waves, an empty boat —
No shock of blond hair glinting in the sun,
No strong, tanned shoulders straining at the oars —
I do not panic, call life guards . . . I know
If I look through glasses, focus carefully,
I'll see, dangling over the side, a young boy hand,
Thin fingers dribbling water now and then,
As Jeb, stretched flat in the bottom, gazes up
Hour after hour into endless blue Maine sky,
Giving Someone up there ample time and space
To fill with shining visions, endless dreams
The empty places in a young boy heart.

HEROES FROM CAMP WINDOWS

For St. John Grenfell Bowron

Small boy has struggled, climbed the highest rock,
Surveys from eight feet up, the whole wide world —
Lake, forest, mountain . . . but what's this? Has he
Like many an older conqueror been caught short?
Unbuckling belt, he casts a covert glance
Toward windows, turns a modest back, drops shorts,
And waters manfully, feet wide apart,
Wild fern and columbine.

                       Quite sure he'll be
Someday a Ph.D., I superimpose
On drooping small white drawers a long black gown,
Top it with velvet hood, and, smiling, spread
Great dollops of red jelly on his bread.

DIVORCE — A LESSON IN VOCABULARY

When I saw the father, body wracked with sobs,
Stand by the window watching the yellow bus
Bring children home from school — but none to him,
Not one, ever again, to run to him,
Paper held high, "Daddy! I got a star!" —
Then I began to understand the word,
The hurt, the pain, the anguish of the word,
The lonely desolation of the word . . . .

And when I saw his great hands clench, unclench
To strike at futile tears, and clench again,
I came at last to comprehend the word,
The never-ending sorrow of the word,
To know the mordant meaning of the word.

HEALING

For Trevanna Frost Grenfell

Trevanna comes with healing in her hands.
Her tiny fingers round his finger curled
Reveal the loving God who understands
A baby's hands can heal a wounded world.

August 31, 1984

THE LONELY COLD

For Tallessyn Zawn Grenfell

My Tallessyn cried when I said goodbye. Big tears
Filled the beautiful brown eyes, hung tremulous,
Rolled slowly down flushed cheeks. **"Grandma,"** *she sobbed,*
"Why — why do you stay such a little time?"

I looked at her, not quite believing. Who
These many years cares when one comes, or when
One goes? But these were honest tears. They flowed
Straight from the heart of the guileless child to mine,
Warmed it against the lonely cold of old.

I held her close, promised to come back soon —
And will remember always . . . Talli cried.

PONY BOY

For Tamarleigh Grace Grenfell

Sometimes in dreams I ride Pony Boy again —
Round and round the track, high up, the wind in my hair . . .
Mommy's there, looking proud, and when we get home, my Dad
Comes bustling in, gives us all big hugs, asks **"How**
Did the lesson go, TG?" *and we all sit down*
Round the table for supper, look up at the blackboard to see
Whose turn for the grace, and it's mine, so we all join hands,
And I say, **"Thank You, God! Thank You, God, for my**
            family!"
Sometimes in dreams I ride Pony Boy again —
Round the track on his back high up the wind in my hair,
Mommy's there, and Dad, and we all join hands for the
            prayer. . . .

CARILLON

For Lieutenant Harvey A. Durant
Corporal William D. Shaw, Jr.
Carman Duncan Walker, MM 2/c USNR

When these bells ring out in praise of Thee,
God of Earth and Sky and Sea,
We shall remember — we gave three . . .

Three who died on earth, sky, sea
Willingly that we might be
Free, O God, to worship Thee.

One fell flaming from the skies.
One beneath the cold sea lies.
One from the earth will never rise.

We shall remember and not forget
Three whom we loved . . . we see them yet . . .
Three whom we owe an unpaid debt —

A debt unpaid till war is done,
A debt unpaid till peace is won,
Owed by the living, every one.

Ring, bells, o'er Bethel hills so fair!
Let holy music fill the air!
Call Bethel folk to bow in prayer!

Sound ancient hymn and carol dear!
Lift up the hearts of all who hear!
Give new courage . . . cast out fear!

Ring, bells, over a land yet free!
Bless, God, the sound in memory
Of three of ours who are with Thee.

Dedication Service
Veterans' Memorial Chime
Bethel, Connecticut
February 11, 1951

COME ALONG, JOSH

A damn health hazard? I understand, sir!
Yes, sir! Right away, sir,
  But if I'd known about this job the day we enlisted . . .
Easy on the gas! Easy does it!
  The day Tom and I sailed over the bay in my boat,
  and Josh came running down to the dock,
  put his foot on the stern . . .
Back it up! Back it up! Can't go at it head on!
How many gears on the damn thing anyway —
  —put his foot on the stern as we shoved off.
  "Room for me?" he grinned.
  "I'm going over to sign up, too,
  now we're graduated."
  I looked at Tom. He was scowling, fumbling with the rope.
  I took a deep breath . . .
Take a deep breath! Not if I can help it!
Not here — not now in this unholy stink —
How many years they been lyin' here anyway?
  "Sorry, Josh," I said, "No room.
  My boat only holds two —" and shoved off,
  leavin' him standing there on the dock
  alone
  the grin gone from his face . . .
Faces! Faces! They got no faces!
Empty eyes and grinnin', grinnin' teeth . . .
Don't grin at me, damn you!
What the hell's so funny? What's the joke?

We picked up the breeze real fast that day,
I felt cold spray on my face,
licked my lips, tasted salt . . .
After awhile I looked back over the wake.
He was still standing on the dock
alone.
Tom saw him, too, and scowled again.
"Damn creep," he said. "Always pushin' in
where he's not wanted
"Yeh," I said. "Always pushin' in . . ."
'Push 'em in, push 'em in!' the Sergeant says.
'Damn health hazard!' the Sergeant says.
'See them big birds up there?' the Sergeant says.
'Well, they ain't chickadees,' the Sergeant says.

Gulls followed us half-way to Portland that day —
the grey gulls of Maine against the grey blue sky . . .
screechin', swoopin', circlin' — hopin' we'd fling
our sandwich crusts on the water . . .
Hundreds of gulls on our island,
hundreds of gulls. . .
but not many Jews. . . not many Jew families
When had Josh come? March?
and followed Tom and me around all spring, hungry
begging the crust of friendship.
They say it's the same other places —
Auschwitz, Buchenwald, Dachou . . .
My friend Josh, where are you now?

I'd have let you come in our boat that day, Josh,
that blue white day
with the white sail scudding over the bay —
I'd have said 'Hop in' and what the hell if Tom scowled
if I'd known about this . . .
I'd sailed three in my boat plenty of times
And you knew it . . . and furthermore,
I'd never have checked
'Mechanically inclined' on that damn form
if I'd known it meant jobs like this . . .

Don't jam, damn you!
What the hell's a bulldozer for if not to bury bones?
Bones, bones, mountains of bones . . .
Nobody in God's world could ever untangle 'em . . .

I was a gravedigger once before
come to think of it . . .
the time we read **Hamlet** in old Smith's class . . .
"Act it out," she said, "in front of the class. . .
You and Tom be the gravediggers. Josh, you be Hamlet . . .
Get down on your hands and knees, boys.
Girls, stop giggling! It's only make-believe!"

We got down on our knees behind her desk for the grave
and all the girls squealed
when we tossed up the skulls —
made 'em in art class for a joke,
wheat paste and wet newspaper —
and old Smith squealed loudest of all
when a wet one landed right in her lap . . .
Funny how women'll squeal over a little thing like that —

Crumple 'em up! Toss 'em away!
Skulls are made of papier mache!
Make-believe, old Smith? What's that you say?
Take another look and gimme an A!
I'm a helluva gravedigger today!

It was Yorick's skull landed in old Smith's lap —
Yorick, the king's funny boy.
I can still see Josh picking up the damn thing,
holding it, tenderly, as if it were alive . . .
"Yorick," he said . . .
and all the girls stopped squealing
and everything was quiet, listening to the voice
of the Jew,
the liquid voice of the Jew . . .
Is that why you hated him, Tom?
'cause he was always Hamlet,
'n you 'n I were only a couple o' gravediggers?
Clowns — they called us in the book. Was that why?

"Alas, poor Yorick," Josh said, in the liquid voice,
"I knew him well . . .
Why, he hath carried me on his back a thousand times . . ."
I knew you, too, Josh, but not very well,
And I wish you'd get the hell off my back!
What are you doing on my back anyway?
It was Hitler killed you, not me!
You and six million like you — Jews!
Every damn Jew he could get his damn hands on . . .
What is a Jew, anyway?
We studied about Jews once in Sunday School . . .
David was a Jew —
the guy with the slingshot who wrote poetry:
'The Lord is my shepherd, I shall not want . . .
He maketh me to lie down in green pastures . . .
He maketh me to lie down in gas chambers . . .
He maketh me to lie down in deep trenches . . .
Surely my trench overfloweth. . .'
That's the last damn pile, soldier.
So pour on the drum o' gasoline, soldier.
But don't toss the match quite yet, soldier,
Till I get the hell outta the way, soldier.
What is a Jew, anyway?
Moses was a Jew, a little Jew kid,
hidin' out on the river so he wouldn't get killed . . .
Auschwitz, Buchenwald, Dachou —
We killed 'em then! We kill 'em now!
Saw a burnin' bush once, Moses did.
Got all excited. Said God
Was inside the bush, inside the burnin' fire . . .
Stick around, Moses! Don't go away!
You'll see more'n a measly bush burnin' in a minute!
You'll see one helluva blaze in a minute!
Stick around! . . . Wow! What a blaze!
Bones, bones burnin' bright
Like a tiger in the night . . .
Who's inside this one, Moses? God? No — not God.
The Devil himself's in this one, Moses —
Adolph 'n Eichmann 'n me 'n the whole rotten world's
in this one! . . . but not God. Not God at all.

I was a Jew once
in the Christmas pageant, the year I was ten.
Had to climb a ladder backstage,
Stick my head out the window way up high.
The Innkeeper — that was me.
Had to holler down to Joseph 'n Mary when they came along
—

"No room! No room for you in this inn!" I said.
"Go somewhere else to be born," I said.
"No room for you in my boat!" I said.
"My boat only holds two —"
And the Christmas angels sang for joy . . .
Herod will kill each little Jew boy . . .
I heard the bells on Christmas Day. . .
Their old familiar carols play . . .
Fly to Egypt! Do not stay!
Christ! What a blaze!
Jesus was a little Jew baby.
Jesus was born a little Jew baby.
"I'll come again," he said.
"I'll come again. Can't say exactly when."
Were you born again, little Jew baby?
In a different town? Dachou, maybe?
Who the hell's buried in this damn trench?
Who the hell's burnin' here anyway?

CHRIST

Come along, Josh . . . get in my boat.
I've carried three in my boat
plenty of times . . .
Come along, Josh . . . please?

Suffield Writers Conference, 1959
Best Stream-of-Consciousness Poem

61

LLOYDIE

Lloydie was different when he came home from the war —
Remote, somehow, as though he'd seen and done
Unfamiliar things the family could never know.
He talked not at all. **"What was it like?"** *I asked.*
"What did you do over there for three long years?"
"It was hot. I ran a bulldozer a lot."
"Digging roads? On South Pacific islands?"
                                                    "No —"
He turned, walked away, turned back, said two short words:
"Digging graves."

                        That was all. Today I look down at his,
At red geraniums, lush grass, or up
At wide blue sky piled high with popcorn clouds,
And think of other days . . .

Red cranberries strung with popcorn, hung on trees,
Dancing to Guy Lombardo New Year's Eve,
Fishing, swimming, laughing with a boy
I knew and loved, the brother with whom I grew
Who went to war — and of a silent man,
A strangely different man I never knew.

NEARLY A YEAR

Nearly a year, nearly a year,
'Missing in action,' nearly a year —
Nearly a year since the great plane fell
Down, down in a flaming hell,
Down, down in a sickening whine
Deep inside the enemy line.

Nearly a year, nearly a year,
Tears have fallen nearly a year —
For every sounding of the phone
Might be a word from the unknown,
For every ringing of the bell
Might be a voice with news to tell.

Nearly a year, nearly a year,
Myriad sounds, but nothing to hear —
***'After a year,'** the letter read,*
'Military declares them dead . . .'
***'Maybe you'd better,'** the family said,*
'Stop worrying now. Think of him dead.'

Nearly a year — but what is a year?
What is a year of hope and fear
When the mother heart within my breast
Will cling to hope until I rest . . .
When eyes will search the empty sky
Until I die . . . until I die . . . .

TWO MINISTERS HAVE I

For H. Bartlett Coffin

Two ministers have I. One wears a robe,
Voluminous and black, wide velvet bands
Up, down, around . . . a purple stole embossed
With crosses, crowns, Greek letters in bright gold.
To those who come a-hungering he serves
The wafer and the wine with quick, deft skill,
Or thunders forth the Word full ominously
From massive pulpit high above the heads
Unnamed, unknown in silent pews below.

This minister is an important man —
Flies to important meetings far and near,
Synods, symposia on world affairs,
Attends important councils everywhere . . .
Buries important people, marries, too,
With ritualistic pomp — but if you, even you,
Should have a problem, you can telephone
His office and his secretary'll look
In her important book and set a time
For an appointment at some future date . . .
If you can wait . . . .

Two ministers have I. The other wears
A faded orange shirt, sits chin in hand
At a kitchen table near an unlocked door
And seldom speaks. He listens, though, listens
To all who come and go, and go and come
Day after day, week after week — the maimed,
The well, the young, the old, the rich, the poor,
Hurting or happy — all who come to sit
At a common table, sharing common things:

The joy when a child is born, the sorrow when
One stumbles and falls . . . pride when some honor's won
Some hard-earned goal attained . . . the deep despair
When the job is lost, the diagnosis not
Benign, the loved one dies, the marriage breaks . . .

He listens, hears the halting words, hears, too,
Unspoken words too difficult to say,
Shares silences, offers the bread, the wine,
The outstretched hand, sometimes the folded bill,
And when tears flow, wipes his own tears away.

So if my heart were breaking, I might go kneel
At an altar rail, take the proffered sacrament
From practiced hands, professional and cool . . .
Or I might walk through an unlocked door to sit
By my minister in the faded orange shirt
Who holds my hand in a warm, unyielding grasp
And lets me know he's been there and he cares.

ROSES IN DECEMBER

The days are closing in, pale narrow days—
Late dawn, a few brief hours, then early dusk . . . .

Here in our northern town the flower shops
Are riotous with color—orange, pink,
Deep purple, lavender, red, yellow, blue—
Last summer's bloom impaled on thin steel wires.
I do not need a dried bouquet, dead flowers.

Pulsing and warm against all darkness, cold,
Vibrant and bright against all sunless hours,
Are memories of those I've loved . . . and so
For living roses here in my December,
I've only to think of you . . . only to remember . . . .

Winter

". . . trees leafless, frozen ruts
Scarring the barren earth, no singing birds."

Photo by Marlene Bridges Smith

THE CARESS AND THE HURT

When I gave you my first poems long ago,
*You wrote these words: **"I love your poetry.***
It strikes some deep-hidden bit of my heart with a touch
That is half a caress, half a hurt. There are few things
That strike that deep . . . but when I read the one —
The one you gave me first down on the bridge —
I felt for a moment as though I must choke. I had
To fight down a lump in my throat that would not go.
Perhaps you can understand . . . can you?"

                                          Of course
I could understand. This was high praise. Your words —
Ingenuous, uncritical, but dear —
Have kept me searching all my life for words
To capture the caress, the hurt life brings . . .

And so — since I can give you little else —
Once more here at the last I give you words.

SOMEONE

Someone remembers you when you were young —
Closes her eyes and sees you hurrying
Along a college walk to take her hand
And run through scurrying leaves for fun.

Someone
Hears laughter echoing across the years
As, lifting her high to keep pink slippers dry,
You stride through drifts of swirling snow.

Someone
Walks time and again with you across the bridge,
Twisting a bit of lilac picked in rain,
Time and again in popcorn-scented dark
Sits marveling at films that talk.

Someone
In sporty little cars with rumble seats
Still rides on summer nights inside your arm
Or waltzes there to medleys long unplayed,
Still dips and sways, still feels on cheek and hair
The brush of lips, whispering you care.

Someone —
Oh, know, my very dear, though time must pass,
The seasons come and go, steps slow, eyes dim—
Someone still sees you in the same old way.
Someone remembers you and loves you still.
Someone remembers you and will until
The fading music dies, the song is sung.
Someone remembers you — gallant, and young!

'DEO VOLENTE . . . PLEASE—'

Today we closed the camp—pulled in the float,
Beached boats, stacked paddles, oars, stored fishing poles,
Dug dahlia bulbs against the killing frost,
Drained pipes, capped chimney tops, swept clean the hearth,
Then groped our way, the windows shuttered tight,
Through darkened, silent rooms, and turned the key.

Today we closed the camp—did once again
Chores done together now year after year,
Chatted and teased, yet each was wondering who—
Each asking the unspoken question, who—
Come spring would fling these bolted shutters wide?
Who kneel to light new fires? launch boats at dawn,
Cast for the wary trout? who dive from the float,
Swim lazily faceup to noonday sun,
To white, unmoving clouds? or paddle out
Halfway across the lake in inky black
To wait the rising moon, to hear loons call,
To drift, to gaze at stars . . . and who—oh, who—
Would plant these shriveled bulbs to bloom again?

Today we closed the camp—each silently
Asking the question, answering silently:
'Let it be us! . . . **Deo volente** *. . . . please—*
Another spring let it still be you and me . . . .'

WE GIVE THEM THINGS

We give them things when they go away. Not for them—
"Take this," we say, "or this, or this, oh, please—
Would you like this plain glass lamp? this silver tray?
There's a story, of course—do you have time to hear?"

We give them things when they go away. Not for them—
"Look around," we say. "Is there something here you'd like?
This old foot tub? this braided rug? It's worn . . .
This vase? this ivory fan? A clipper ship
Once carried it halfway around the world . . .
There's a story, of course—do you have time to hear?"

We give them things when they go away—not for them,
But for ourselves! "Take this!" we say. "Oh, please—
Into your distant life far down the years
Take some small part of mine! Remember me!
Give it some day to some child yet unborn.
Give it and say, 'She gave me this one day
As I was going away.' Say, 'There's a story, of course . . .
Do you have time—do you have time to hear?'"

SET OUT THE CUPS

When I get home, I thought, I'll make the tea.
I'll put the kettle on, set out the cups —
Yours white, mine blue — and then we'll sit and talk
About the service . . .

How the people sang
The 'Alleluias' in your favorite hymn!
How blue the heather was — almost as blue
As that you picked in Cornwall long ago
And tucked into my hair! And how our son,
So like you, made them laugh (Imagine that!)
With loving stories of his dad, and how
The gentle scent of roses followed us
As we filed out to stand among the stones . . .

When I get home, when I get home, I thought,
I'll make the tea, we'll sit for hours and chat.
I'll put the kettle on, set out the cups —
Set out the cups . . .

no, put the white one back.

"DON'T CRY!"

He cried easily those last few years — the sound
Of the children's voices on the telephone,
A hymn his mother sang, an old snapshot,
My hand on his in a crowded restaurant —
"Don't cry!" I'd say impatiently. **"Oh, please —
Don't cry!"**
                    Retired — pride, vigor, usefulness
All gone — he laid the masks aside and cried.

'Second childhood,' some would say, and in a way
He was a child, more sensitive, his 'heart
Upon his sleeve,' more easily hurt or pleased . . .

Like a child he'd bring the first half-open bloom
From the lilac hedge, hold it delightedly
Under my nose, say **"Smell!"** Or shuffle out
Day after day in June until he'd found
On unpruned bushes planted long ago,
A stunted rose . . . **"Don't cry! Oh, please — don't cry!"**

Don't cry . . . I tell myself, longing to see
Those childlike tears . . . have rosebuds brought to me . . .

UNLESS —

He held their hands in his
Year after year after year
In hospitals, in homes
In car, in ambulance, beside the road
Held firm their dying hands
And comforted, heard prayers:
**'Yea, though I walk through the valley,
Thou art with me . . .'**
**'Though I take the wings of the morning,
Thou art there . . .'**

And no one there —
Not wife, not child,
Not doctor, nurse, friend, priest
Not even stranger —
There
To hold his hand, to hear the prayer . . .

I see
His great kind caring ministering hand
Reaching out in darkness
Groping
Growing cold
Unheld, uncomforted . . .
Unless —
Unless —

O God, was Someone there
To hold his hand, to hear the prayer?

PEREGRINE WIDOW

*"**Where is your home?**" they ask — strangers, polite,*
*Well-meaning, wanting to be kind. "**Where do***
You live?" "Where are you from?"
                                        I do not know.
I am from a husband's heart that held me close
Long years and holds me now no more. I am from
The life, the love we shared, the homes, the rooms
Where laughter rang and tears were kissed away,
From rocking chairs where lullabies were sung
And small ones comforted, from fires that burn,
From flowers that bloom no longer, candlelight
On tables set with silver, altar rails
Where hands I knew broke the forgiving bread —
I am from all these, for they are gone away,
Receded quite, all passed . . . and I am from . . .

*"**Where are you from?**" they ask. "**Where do you live?**"*
*They ask and ask again, "**Where is your home?**"*
There is no home — an address, yes, a house,
Table and chair and bed and board, but when
The heart is homeless, then there is no home,
And I am from . . .

                    *"**Where are you from?**" "**Where is***
Your home?" "Where do you live?"
                                        I do not live,
But go through motions only day by day —
Rise up, lie down, walk, talk, say 'yea' and 'nay' —
Living is something I did yesterday.
I am from . . . I am from . . . I am from . . . I am away.

                    Kansas City
                    Christmas, 1981

'THE STUFF THEY SELL'

Today they put the **FOR SALE** sign on the lawn —
Came early, pounded in the pointed stakes,
And left without a word.
                              I watched through a blur
Of sudden, unexpected tears . . . **FOR SALE**
Was it old Khayyam wondered *'what they buy*
One-half so precious as the stuff they sell'?

'The stuff they sell —'
                              White lilacs bending low
Along the hedge, red tulips trumpeting . . .
In May around the bird bath, violets
That two small girls knelt patiently to pick
Each Mother's Day . . . pink petals fluttering down
From apple, dogwood, pear tree all in bloom . . .
One shy, brown cottontail we called Bryl Creme . . .
The mourning doves' complaint, my cardinal,
A flash of red against the giant pine
Where Rebel lay, head down, disconsolate,
September days when all trooped off to school . . .

'The stuff they sell' —
                              Twin lions standing guard,
Stout British sentinels . . . inside the door
"The house still smells the same!" the children say
On brief, infrequent visits from away . . .
Children with children now, amazed to find
The half-forgotten smell of home unchanged —
Pizza and chocolate chips, warm redolence
Of turkey stuffed with Bell's . . . Pam's yellow bread,
Great fragrant loaves of saffron, baked for Dad . . .
The Easter lily Doran's always sent,
Pungent and piercing sweet . . . the bearskin rug
Before the fire, burnt marshmallows, green boughs
From balsam Christmas trees exploding sparks
That shot our Twelfth Night prayers straight up to God . . .

'The stuff they sell —'
                        Remembered voices, sounds . . .
Laughter and hymns and always poetry
*Easing the irksome task . . . blue **Sound and Sense***
*Propped open by the sink — **'And hast thou slain***
The Jabberwock?'** . . . **'It is morning, Senlin says . . .'
*And **'When, oh, when shall we three meet again. . .'***
Parties to say farewell to comrades, friends,
To teachers, preachers, soldiers, sailors — then
Parties to welcome home again . . . birthdays
With candle-dripping cakes, Hall-Conard kids,
Their blue or crimson jackets wet with snow,
Crashing in droves when Lorni turned sixteen,
*The driveway jammed with cars. **"I didn't know***
My daughter had so many friends! I'll go
***For Coke!"** John's Slingerland, the flying sticks,*
*The thumping bass — **"Gonna rock around the clock***
Tonight, gonna rock, gonna rock, in my blue suede shoes . . ."
The piano painted pink . . . the rumpus room
Alive with noise . . .

          Then four November days
When all, transfixed before the screen, met death . . .
Immobilized and mute, except for Pam
Who crept away between dry sobs to write
Her anguished verse . . .

The rooms all tidy now . . . no wild array
Of dog collection, tutus, ballet shoes,
No skis, no skates, no flying flat white seeds
From Jack o' Lanterns scooped with careless haste . . .
Beneath the warming lamp no wild duck eggs
For science project . . . gerbil, mouse, long gone . . .
No frenzied midnight sewing for the prom,
The play . . . no cardboard angel wings to spray
Bright gold . . .

              The rooms all silent now except
For the lingering sound of pounding echoing still
From hammered stakes sunk deep into the lawn —
The long green sloping lawn where once we raked
Great heaps of scarlet leaves against the wind
And ran and jumped and shouted Shelley's **Ode** *—*
'Yellow, and black, and pale, and hectic red,
Pestilence-stricken multitudes —' *and raked*
And ran and leaped again and laughed and loved
As if life stayed forever young, unchanged . . .
As if green lawns stayed always fresh and green . . .
As if leaves never fell . . . nor sudden tears . . .
Nor men . . . as if . . . as if . . .

Today they put the **FOR SALE** *sign on the lawn.*

LEAVING THE PARSONAGE

The van has left. Pale sunbeams pierce the gloom
Of thick-leafed maples and the one pine tree.
Walk once more through each strangely tidy room,
Clicking the shutter of dear memory.

Five Christmases we had the tree just there . . .
How well the plants did on that window sill . . .
Jill helped me paint this old red rocking chair . . .
My sister's hands are idle now, and still . . .

***"Let's have a service,"** John would always say,*
Lighting the taper with elaborate care . . .
***"Pass out the hymnals —"** See the hallowed play*
Of candlelight on small heads bowed in prayer . . .

*God bless who comes . . . **"Yes, dear, a minute more —"***
God bless who leaves . . . walk softly . . . close the door.

THERE IS NO ONE THERE

Why are you driving so fast? There is no one there—
No one watching, waiting to call, "I'm glad you're home!"
The storm's so bad I've been worried about you, dear!"

Why are you driving so fast? Did you forget?
Did you think for a moment things are as they used to be—
Every window ablaze with light, the door flung wide,
Voices and laughter and love flowing out, "Mom's here . . .
Hi, Mom! Supper's ready . . . we've all been waiting for you!"

Why are you driving so fast? The house will be dark . . .
The mail still there in the box at the foot of the drive . . .
You'll fumble to fit the key, flick on the lights . . .
The stove will be cold, no kettle bubbling for tea . . .
Your coffee mug unwashed on the shelf by the sink . . .

Why are you driving so fast? There is no one there.
Slow down . . . slow down . . . There is no one waiting for you.

SOME OTHER, BRAVER DAY

Dull winter day . . . no sun . . . a threatening pall
Of clouds . . . a day, perhaps, to shop the mall,
To wander aimlessly . . . .
                              But don't stop there
By racks of lacy cards for those who care
Enough to send the very best. Walk fast . . .
And look the other way as you walk past
Red satin candy boxes, each a heart.
A goldfoil Cupid with a paper dart
Can make tears start . . . .
                              Don't stop to finger ties,
And smoothing rough tweed jackets isn't wise,
Nor lingering near high piles of sailing gear—
Who needs a jaunty Captain's cap this year?

Don't ask about a special blend of tea . . .
Nor pause to browse through books about the sea—
White gulls and scudding sails and surf . . .
                              Don't gaze
At rings and things seen through a salty haze—
Easy enough to say that diamonds last
Forever when forever doesn't last . . .

Walk fast . . . look for an exit . . . down this way—
Come shop the mall some other, braver day.

                    February 14, 1984

LETTER

Isn't it strange —
How your remembered script, so long unseen,
Can startle, make the heart beat faster, take
Me decades back in one quick glance to young —
Not mother, wife, grandmother, only young . . .
Untouched, your hands still shyly tentative . . .
Lips innocent, unkissed . . . all unexplored,
Unlived, the pulse to come . . .

Isn't it strange —
How such a common thing, plain white, addressed
In ordinary blue, postmarked in black,
Can change slow steps that cautious creep about
To flying feet of schoolgirl, racing home
To find this in the post . . .

Isn't it strange —
The way you write my name can move me still,
Each upward stroke, each curve call back the hands
That stroked each curve . . .

Now break the seal. Take out
The pages that suffice to tell a life —
Advanced degree, long marriage, work, the war,
Vacations, travel, health — recounted here
With courteous restraint, as to someone
Remote . . . almost unknown . . . a stranger, yes —
We've lived our lives apart. I watch the sun
Rise each day from one sea. You watch it sink
Into another. Still — is it not strange
That for a little space of glad surprise
Your old familiar writing could blot out
The miles, the years, efface dull age, erase
Both time and space?

Dear long-ago first love,
Is it not strange — and strangely wonderful —
That flesh does not forget, remembers yet?
That love, once freely given, does not die?
Lives on unfed . . . unnurtured still endures?

TOUCH

You have not touched my hand in many years
Nor smoothed my hair nor brushed away my tears,
But, when the letters come, I lay my face
On letters your familiar hand has traced
And almost feel across long years, far lands
The still-remembered touch, the gentle hands.

KEY

"Keep this until I come again," *you said*
And pressed into my hand a small gold key,
Emblazoned with a tree, and went away
And did not come again.

       Long years it lay
Against the velvet of my jewel box —
Unclaimed, unworn, unused.

       Who would have thought
This small gold key had power to unlock
A friendship frozen in oblivion,
Leap decades of divergence, reconcile
Two hearts — grown older, wiser — each to each?

CONDOLENCE CALL

*Just driving through, he says, **happened to hear***
That she's a widow now . . . so grieved, so sad . . .
But sympathizes . . . lost his own dear wife
Short weeks ago . . .

They sit on the sofa . . . talk . . .
His hand on the empty cushion there between,
Pink palm upturned, pink fingers slightly curled . . .

She knows that hand! Her cheek, her hair, her breast
All know from long ago its tender stroke,
Its lingering, soft caress . . . and now she wants
So much, so very much, to reach across
The sofa cushion there, to feel again
The throb, the pulse, the old familiar touch . . .

She grips her hands together, clenches tight,
The knuckles turning white . . . listens and chats,
Remembers to say thanks for stopping by . . .

And tries to smile, or at least tries not to glare,
At the new wife sitting there in the opposite chair.

CHARRED LOGS

"Are you happy, dear?" he asks. She sits on the rug,
Head against his knee . . . his fingers now and then
Touching her hair . . . The fire burns low—charred logs,
Too far apart, too separate . . . Soon, she knows,
He'll stand, take tongs in hand, lift gently till
The black sticks, side by side, blaze up again . . .

Could people do the same—old people, charred
With living, separate, alone? Could they
Ignite new fires for comfort? warmth? for light
On the darkening way?

　　　　　　　　　To her left the ribboned bow,
The jeweler's box . . . to her right the tiny vase
Of woodland flowers she'd watched him bend to pick
Columbine, Star of Bethlehem—then give to her
With a grin still boyish, young . . .
　　　　　　　　　　　　They'd shared a meal,
White candles gleaming soft on the crocheted cloth
Brought when he cleared away his mother's things.
He'd cooled champagne, proposed a toast: **"To all
The years behind and all the years ahead!"**

"Are you happy, dear?" he asks again. She turns,
Looks up into his face—the same dear face
She'd known long years ago when all was young . . .
Wishes with all her heart she could answer 'Yes,
Oh, yes, I'm happy—happy, dear!' . . . but no—

Happy's a word for another, vanished day . . .
Not in his power to give . . . or take away.

WORDS, LONG AFTER

So we meet on a summer night as the music plays
At a place where the music played long years ago . . .
A place where we danced at a ball long years ago . . .
"Isn't this nice!" *you say, guiding our steps*
Along shadowed walks across the patio,
Old people, moving cautiously and slow . . .
Then, pride in your voice, **"I want you to meet my son!"**

I see a smiling man, a face I know . . .
Dark eyes alight with whimsey, wit . . . the same
Lopsided grin I traced with fingertips
As we laughed and loved at a ball long years ago . . .
As you whispered words at a ball long years ago . . .
"Your father sent me your picture once," *I say,*
"On a Christmas card . . . was it thirty years ago?
You were wearing your Dr. Denton's—"

                                                            I hold out my hand . . .

But echoing there in the night are other words,
Words heard as the music played long years ago . . .
Words heard as you held me close long years ago . . .
   'I can't imagine anyone else but you
   Mother of my children—no one else but you . . . .'

Now your son holds my hand, and I look at him,
                longing to say:
"Come close! Oh, please—do you know me? I am the one—
Let me touch your face!—the one who might have been . . ."

But he drops my hand, for he does not know, and you
Have forgotten, too, words said when all was new:
   'I can't imagine anyone else but you—'
Words said as the music played long years ago . . .
Words said as we danced at a ball long years ago . . .
As I danced in your arms at a ball long years ago . . . .

SOMEHOW I ALWAYS THOUGHT

Somehow I always thought you'd come again . . .
One winter day, perhaps—I'd see you stride
Across some crowded airport, bag in hand,
Eyes searching till you found me, or some spring
You'd swing into my drive, sit grinning there
Behind the wheel till I flung wide the door
And bade you in . . . somehow I always thought . . .

Somehow I always thought you'd come again . . .
In summertime or some bright day in fall . . .
We'd walk and talk and laugh and go again
To places that we knew and know again
The peace and joy not ever known elsewhere . . .

Somehow I always thought—until today.
Your name, your face here on the page . . . long list
Of great accomplishments, all duly praised,
The many things you did all eulogized,
All known, all noted here . . . except for two—
The two I knew . . .
                          you loved me, went away,
And did not, will not ever, come again.

THE WARM NEVER QUITE GOES AWAY

The old lady walks,
leaning heavily on her cane,
from Fernald, where the bookstore used to be
past Carnegie, where the library used to be
to Balentine, still a women's dormitory . . .
drops her cane, sinks gratefully to the lowest granite step,
draws a deep breath,
lets the breeze lift her hair
lets the April sun warm her. . . .

Girls, arms full of books, come and go
from class, to class, chatter, laugh,
leap steps, two at a time . . .
Now a girl and a boy come along,
pause . . . he leaning against the rail,
she on the topmost step.
Not wanting to leave each other,
they talk, laugh, are silent . . .
look deeply into each other's eyes . . .
let the breeze lift their hair,
let the April sun warm them. . . .

The old lady listens to the silence, turns.
"Would you like to hear a poem?" *she asks.*
Startled, they glance for the first time
at the bundle of clothes on the bottom step . . .
faded eyes, wrinkled skin, wooden cane . . .
relic from another world
breaking into theirs.
They look at each other. The boy nods.

So the old lady tells them a poem
about a boy and a girl
who walked one day
from Fernald when it was still the bookstore
past Carnegie when it was still the library
to Balentine, the women's dormitory
and how they, too, paused on the steps,
reluctant to leave each other,
talked, laughed, and were silent,
looked deeply into each other's eyes,
let the breeze lift their hair,
let the April sun warm them . . .

"Did you marry him?" *the girl asks into the silence.*
"No —" *the old lady grasps the rail, pulls herself up.* **"No—he
married someone else."**
"Oh —" *Again they look at each other. Can it be love does not
last forever?*
"And did you?" *The boy, wanting to get it straight, reaches
down, hands her the cane.*
"Marry someone else? Yes, I did, too."
Then, seeing disappointed faces, the old lady smiles.
"But the warm—the warm never quite goes away."

MY ROCK

When I was nine, my grandmother took my hand,
Walked me beside the sea, gave me a rock—

"This is your rock," she said. "You must know it well.
A glacier carried it five thousand miles
From Hudson Bay, perhaps from the very Pole,
Then dropped it here for me to give to you.
Oh, yes, perhaps some Indian girl once climbed
Its granite sides, lay on it, called it hers,
And perhaps long years from now some other girl
May claim it for her own. But for your life,
Your little span of years, this rock is yours.
Now scramble up . . . ."
                                          "Does it have a name?" I asked.
"A secret name—some call it Work, some Truth,
Some call it Love—but you'll not know its name
Till you are old and have built your life on it.
Now lie face down. Do you see the tiny specks,
Bright crystals shining in the sun? That's quartz.
You'll study rocks in school someday. Turn now
And face the sky. Spread wide your arms. Do you feel
The rock beneath you—hard, unyielding, firm?

Say: This is the rock my grandmother gave to me."
This is the rock my grandmother gave to me.
"Through every shifting sand that I must walk,"
Through every shifting sand that I must walk,
"This rock will hold me up. This is my rock."
This rock will hold me up. This is my rock.

When I was nine, my grandmother took my hand,
Walked me beside the sea, gave me a rock . . . .

ALWAYS HERE

Always here — the lake, the hills, the sky . . .
Sweet smell of pine cones, roasting in the sun . . .
Always here — the lone loon's aching cry . . .
Twin stars, above, below, when day is done . . .

Always here — the peepers' symphony,
The circling gulls, the eagles' swooping flight . . .
Always here — the lilies' mystery,
Up from black mud come blooms of purest white . . .

When far away in cities built by man,
Man's suffering, sin, and sorrow ever near,
I shall be glad, remembering again,
The lake, the hills, the sky are always here.

Plantation 33
Long Pond, Maine, 1937

WISH

I wish someone would come along and fling
An arm around my shoulders, leave it there
Awhile, unthinkingly, till I reach up
And press a hand, a hand that presses back . . .

Nothing I touch responds — not wooden arms
On rocking chair . . . not stiff, unbending cane
I lean upon . . . not plastic switches, knobs
On TV, clock, lamp, radio . . . not locks
On windows, nor the chain I fasten tight
Across the door at night . . .
                              Nothing I touch
Touches me back with pat, hug, kiss, caress,
With quick embrace, spontaneous and warm . . .

I wish . . . I wish someone would fling an arm
Around my shoulders, leave it there awhile,
Careless and kind, till I reach up and press
A hand — a hand that pulses, presses back . . . .

COMMUNION AT THORNTON HEIGHTS

This is the place where I am most at home,
Am most at peace, most nearly my own self,
The place — though I may not know a name, a face —
Where I lean back on my own family,
Lean back on God . . . look up through vaulted space
Above the altar there, the wine, the bread,
And feel myself uplifted, nurtured, fed
On grace. This is the place, the place.

                                       I hear
Around me all the rise and fall of sound,
Cadence of murmured prayer, petition, praise,
The pulse of organ, anthem, soaring hymn:
"Lift up your hearts! We lift them up . . ."

                                       Silent,
Myself too maimed for words, I listen for
The timeless words that minister to me:
"Ye that do truly, earnestly repent . . .
Give us this day . . . my body, broken for thee . . ."
No sham, pretense . . . all, all are sinners here —
"Not worthy so much as to gather up the crumbs" —
Humble before a God who knows, yet loves,
Who judges, yet absolves, and most of all
Gives courage to go on — ". . .*that ye may walk*
In newness of life, may grow, may dwell in him."

                                   In all the world
This is the place where I am most at peace,
Am most myself, the self I want to be.
This place in all the world is home to me.

GRAVESEND

Why are we stopping here? I asked.
Gravesend? I don't remember this station . . .

    End o' the line, bawled the Conductor.
    Ev'rybody out . . . end o' the line line line
But it can't be, I said.
I meant to get off at Penn, buy roses.
They're lovely there in June, long stems . . .

    Move along, Lady, yelled the Conductor.
    Move along long long
What do you mean, pushing me off in this rude way?
It hasn't been a long ride at all,
and there's a friend near 59th I meant to visit long ago . . .
When did we pass the 59th Street station?

    Long ago go go, chanted the Conductor
    Go along now, Lady, go go go
I intended to stop at Llewisohn, too, I said,
spend considerable time listening to the music . . .
and there's a church near Riverside—
I was going there to say a prayer . . .

    There there there, sang the Conductor
    Gravesend Station, we're there there there
Is this an express train? I asked.
The ride seems over so fast.
I know I started on a local, stopping here and there . . .
        along the way . . .
my friends, and the flowers, and the music . . .
Is this an express?
Did I change to an express?

    Press press press, hissed the Conductor
    to the end end end
    end o' the line, Lady, ev'rybody out Gravesend
I'm so surprised . . .
No, don't bother with parcels . . .
but there were so many places I meant to stop
along the way . . . .

'. . . TILL DEATH DO US PART'

Into the emptiness between us now,
Into the void, immeasurable and wide,
I fling these words to ease the severed vow,
Knowing that words and words alone abide.

ABOUT THE AUTHOR . . .

Clarine Coffin Grenfell is a native of Bangor, Maine, but has spent much of her adult life as educator and writer in New York and Connecticut. She earned her Bachelor of Arts degree with Phi Beta Kappa honors at University of Maine and her Bachelor of Divinity at Hartford Theological Seminary. At various times she has been the pastor of Methodist churches, chairperson of departments of English, editor and reading consultant in the Educational Division of *Reader's Digest*. Married for many years to the late Reverend Jack Grenfell, she is the mother of a son and two daughters.

A popular speaker throughout her career, she especially enjoys traveling the country and sharing her 'prose and verse' with live audiences. Since 1982 these audiences have totaled more than fourteen thousand people of all ages, plus an uncounted number via radio and television. If you would like to order books or to invite Mrs. Grenfell to come to your school, church, library, or club, you may write to Grenfell Reading Center, Orland, Maine 04472.